The mind of a curious soul

Jagdish Kaur Bansil

BookLeaf Publishing
India | USA | UK

Presentation by *BookLeaf Publishing*

Web: www.bookleafpub.com

E-mail: info@bookleafpub.com

ISBN: 978-93-5761-153-4

First edition 2022

DEDICATION

I feel the acknowledgments say most of what I feel about this incredible opportunity I was given. I hope that whoever reads these poems, finds inspiration, comfort, and joy from these words. I guess I'd like to dedicate the book to every single person who reads it.

ACKNOWLEDGEMENT

Firstly, I'd like to thank Bhai Sahib Bhai Mohinder Singh Ji, who have showered their divine blessings on me from the day I was born. Without their guidance, none of this would have been possible.
Then I'd like to thank my parents who continue to encourage me and help me to achieve my dream. They are my greatest fans and give me the confidence to reach for the stars.
I have two wonderful younger brothers, Gopal and Harjot, who make me laugh and make me happy. They even inspired me with these poems. I'd also like to thank the rest of my family who have given me lots of love and support.

PREFACE

I love reading books. At school, English has always been my favourite subject, which is why I have developed a keen interest in writing. I told my daddy that I want to write a book one day. My daddy said to me "Why one day? Why not today?". So here I am, at the beginning of my writing journey.

My dream life

At the beginning of my dream,
I laugh and sing and play.
Maybe now or every day I'll play like this if I
may.

Now I have to protect my elders,
No laugh and sing and play.
I have to take it seriously,
For Coronavirus is on its way.

Wisdom

Wisdom can come from your elders.
It's them who empower you,
So listen, learn and live by their stories.
Don't deny their words.
Obey!
Make your life enjoyable, but listen to them for
you can achieve great things.

Oceans of thought

It feels like the world is crying out to us,
People acting normal, not giving a fuss.
But there are those that genuinely care,
Breaking rules like it's a dare.

What can we do to make things right?
Technology is advancing, the future is bright.
We must make better decisions on the things we buy,
Whilst scientists figure a better way to fly.

So let's unite together on this journey as one,
Let's start taking action as this poem is done.

Hedgehogs

Hedgehog; as spiky as a conker, as splintery as a
log.
Every autumn, every fall,
  the hoglets decide to come and crawl.
  Begging for berries so juicy and sweet.
  Oh, how they wish for a little treat.
Don't go little creatures,
  we love your adorable features.
Great gardener's friend,
  they're happy to lend
  lots of caterpillars, bugs, and worms.
Erinaceus europaeus - it's in the name,
  they have a range of homes.
  All naturally grown burrows, hedges, and
forests.
Hibernating in the cold weather,
  snuggling up tight together.
One on the red list,
  soon to be extinct.
Gone, gone, gone!
  They are now extinct!
So hear me out,
  do you want these burrow diggers, spiky
figures, prickly creatures, owners of adorable
features, forever gone?

Time

Time is valuable
Time is precious
You can't buy time
It's limited
So get up!
Get up and make a difference before it's too late
Time is an hourglass
Except you don't know how long you've got!

Caterpillar

Small and timid, I wriggle through battles.
Big and strong, I break through the shackles.
I am tired now, for I must rest.
Tomorrow brings a new test.
Tomorrow brings new light.
My new wings, carry me high to shine bright.
I am free.
I am me.

Dreams

I wish upon a star.
I try to think hard,
But I don't need to look far
Because all my aspirations and ambitions
Are near and dear.

The Rain

The whole world is magical,
So big yet so small.
So many wrong-doings,
The earth will crumble, the earth will fall.
The whole world is raining,
Eyes brimming with tears.
Earth crumbling like it's hailing,
This will be everyone's greatest fear.

The Loving Astronaut

I climb up high,
Going beyond the sky.
Looking down,
At the creations they've found.
Longing to go back,
Even though I fear they'll lack
The love and compassion,
That will keep everything going.

Windmill

I spin and spin and spin,
Somehow I just can't win.
For something is weighing me down.
Fear!
I must release it now.
I try and try, but I wonder how.
How will I let my fears out?
And not let them push me about.
I am now free.

Eternal

Roses are beautiful,
So soft to touch.
When they are gifted,
They mean so much.

Such simple flowers,
Last many hours.
They always bring delight and joy,
Not one can destroy.

Childhood

Sunshine, sunshine, you bring me joy.
Sunshine, sunshine, you're fun like a toy.

Children come and play.
When you're out, they shout hooray!

You're part of our life,
Without you, there'll be strife.

Sunshine, sunshine, you bring me joy.
Sunshine, sunshine, you're fun like a toy.

Tree

There was a tree that had a twig
And on the twig, there was a fig.
The tree was tall,
So you had to knock the fruit off with a ball
But beware you don't get bitten by an ear-wig!

Spring

Blossoms are blooming
Colours so mesmerising
They're rich and fragrant

Foxgloves and daisies
And all the other flowers
Spring is on its way

Chicks and lamb are born
New life at the break of dawn
Chicks tweet and lamb bleat

Spring is coming soon
I can smell it in the air
Spring is in the air

Have you gone bananas?

Banana, banana,
Looks like a smile.
Banana, banana,
Can make you walk for a while.

Banana, banana,
Yellow like the Sun.
Banana, banana
Yum yum in my tum.

Banana, banana
So lovely and sweet
Banana, banana,
My favourite squishy treat.

Banana, banana
My brother doesn't like you!

Sunshine

It's a happy day,
Go run, run.
It's a sunny day,
Have fun, fun.

We go out to play,
In different ways.
We play with water guns,
We have so much fun with everyone!

Bubbles
I've been cast away in a bubble,
No fear, no anger, no trouble.

I've been cast away into a magical land,
It's my dreamland.

I feel ecstatic, for my one dream has come true,
I now have the power to do what I do.

Bubbles

I've been cast away in a bubble,
No fear, no anger, no trouble.

I've been cast away into a magical land,
It's my dreamland.

I feel ecstatic, for my one dream has come true,
I now have the power to do what I do.

Beside the Seaside

Sunny skies, glistening sea.
Warm, golden sand,
Ice cream melting in my hand.
The seagulls fly gracefully.

I feel the warmth against my skin,
Before the cool breeze hits me.
The red crabs run free,
Just like it's supposed to be.

Sandcastles are being made,
Picnics blankets and sandwiches are being laid.
Buckets and spades in the sun,
Everyone is having fun.

Oceans

I weep oceans of tears
For they kill these significant creatures
Cuttlefish are used for clothing dyes
Fish are killed to eat
Unfortunately!
I weep oceans of tears
For they kill these significant creatures

Jagdish

Joy is what I like to spread,
Ambition is in my heart and head.
Generous is how we should really be,
Diligence is in the essence of me.
I've got so much I want to achieve,
Sure I can, as long as I believe.
Holy Lord, please guide me.

www.ingramcontent.com/pod-product-compliance
Lightning Source LLC
LaVergne TN
LVHW011310210726
843509LV00017B/3017